UNCOVERING THE JAMESTOWN COLONY

Please visit our website, www.garethstevens.com. For a free color catalog of all our high-quality books, call toll free 1-800-542-2595 or fax 1-877-542-2596.

Library of Congress Cataloging-in-Publication Data

Names: McAneney, Caitie, author.
Title: Uncovering the Jamestown Colony / Caitie McAneney.
Description: New York : Gareth Stevens Publishing, [2017] | Series: Hidden history | Includes index.
Identifiers: LCCN 2016027687| ISBN 9781482458060 (pbk. book) | ISBN 9781482458077 (6 pack) | ISBN 9781482458084 (library bound book)
Subjects: LCSH: Jamestown (Va.)–History–17th century–Juvenile literature. | Virginia–History–Colonial period, ca. 1600-1775–Juvenile literature.
Classification: LCC F234.J3 M26 2017 | DDC 975.5/4251–dc23
LC record available at https://lccn.loc.gov/2016027687

First Edition

Published in 2017 by
Gareth Stevens Publishing
111 East 14th Street, Suite 349
New York, NY 10003

Designer: Katelyn E. Reynolds
Editor: Therese Shea

Photo credits: Cover, pp. 1, 7, 9, 15, 19 (inset), 23 (both), 25, 29 (main) MPI/Getty Images; cover, pp. 1–32 (tear element) Shahril KHMD/Shutterstock.com; cover, pp. 1–32 (background texture) cornflower/Shutterstock.com; cover, pp. 1–32 (background colored texture) K.NarlochLiberra/Shutterstock.com; cover, pp. 1–32 (photo texture) DarkBird/Shutterstock.com; cover, pp. 1–32 (notebook paper) Tolga TEZCAN/Shutterstock.com; p. 5 Stock Montage/Getty Images; pp. 11, 27 courtesy of the Library of Congress; p. 13 Archive Photos/Getty Images; p. 17 Linda Davidson/The Washington Post via Getty Images; p. 19 (main) Ira Block/National Geographic/Getty Images; p. 21 Hulton Archive/Getty Images; p. 29 (inset) Bill O'Leary/The Washington Post via Getty Images.

Printed in the United States of America

CPSIA compliance information: Batch #CW17GS: For further information contact Gareth Stevens, New York, New York at 1-800-542-2595.

CONTENTS

Words in the glossary appear in **bold** type
the first time they are used in the text.

THE HIDDEN TRUTH

Jamestown is known as the first permanent English settlement in North America, but underneath the well-known history is a darker past. In its beginning years, the settlement was far from successful. In fact, most colonists who came to Jamestown never left—they died shortly after arriving.

Jamestown was a settlement in the Virginia colony. The Virginia Company of London established it in 1607. The company hoped to make a profit in the New World. They expected to find riches, especially gold, and enough land for anyone who wanted it.

What the colonists found was far from what they'd imagined. Read on to learn more about what actually happened at Jamestown and the hidden truth about the near failure of America as we know it.

REVEALED

Jamestown colonists were supposed to settle the land, strike gold, and find a waterway to the Pacific Ocean for trade.

FAILURE AT ROANOKE

Jamestown wasn't the first English settlement. That title goes to Roanoke, which the English established in 1585 on an island off the coast of modern North Carolina. That attempt failed, and colonists tried to settle there again in 1587. Soon after, their leader, John White, returned to England for supplies. By the time he came back in 1590, his people had disappeared, leaving behind only the word "Croatoan." The disappearance of the Roanoke colonists continues to be a great mystery.

Hostile native peoples, unfamiliar land, and harsh winters were just some of the challenges the Roanoke colonists faced.

A BIG MISTAKE

The Jamestown colonists made the long journey from England on three ships: *Discovery*, *Susan Constant*, and *Godspeed*. There were 104 men and boys on board, and they intended to start a settlement—one that would last.

On May 13, 1607, the ships arrived at a location on the James River. There were no native peoples living there, and it was far enough away from the ocean to protect them from Spanish naval attacks. In many ways, this seemed ideal. However, it was far from perfect.

Native peoples chose not to live in the Jamestown area for a reason. It was marshy and wet. Colonists were close to water, but it wasn't always healthy to drink.

REVEALED

One reason Jamestown colonists chose the location was for the deep water nearby. They could tie their ships to trees.

BUILDING JAMESTOWN

The Jamestown settlement was a triangle-shaped fort. It had a bulwark at each point. A bulwark is a strong wall for protection. There were little houses and dwellings within the walls for the colonists. How do we know what Jamestown looked like? Archaeologist William Kelso started excavating the site in 1994. His team found proof that Jamestown existed there, and over many years, they also found wells, graves, and building foundations.

When the colonists claimed their land, they named it after King James I.

NATIVE LAND

Many people imagine the Jamestown colonists landing in a wild place once they reached America. They imagine overgrown forests and as much land as the colonists wanted, right at their feet. This is far from the truth.

In reality, the colonists arrived to a land that was already well settled by native peoples. About 14,000 Algonquian-speaking people lived in the area. It was part of the huge empire of Tsenacomoco, which was broken into villages with hundreds of people apiece. They cleared the forests by burning the trees, and they made huge cornfields. They had an advanced system of farming, which involved using land for a while and then leaving it to recover. The native people were experts on farming and living in this area.

REVEALED

In the beginning, Powhatan and his people traded with the English. They gave the colonists land in exchange for valuable guns, beads, and metal tools.

POWHATAN

The leader of Tsenacomoco was Wahunsenacah, a strong and able chief. He's better known today as Chief Powhatan, after the name of his people. When Powhatan was a young man, he gained power over an empire made up of six tribes. He **incorporated** many more tribes into the empire. It was a successful union, and he was the chief of all chiefs. When the English first arrived, Powhatan didn't lead any great attacks against them. He probably thought they'd die out on their own. He would change his mind later on.

Although Powhatan and his people didn't attack at first, their relationship with the colonists later became violent.

A ROCKY START

If Powhatan believed Jamestown would fail, he was nearly correct. Many of the 104 men and boys who arrived in Jamestown died quickly. In fact, by January 1608, only 38 were left.

Jamestown was originally led by a council of seven colonists. The colony needed a strong leader if it could ever survive. John Smith rose to the call. Smith was an English soldier and explorer. He wasted no time in exploring the area. He traveled to native villages to find food for his people. On one of his expeditions, Smith was captured and nearly killed. Once Smith was freed, he returned to Jamestown. He made sure his men—hungry and thirsty as they were—were working. He said, "He that will not work will not eat."

REVEALED

There was a great amount of fish in the James River for colonists to catch. Archaeologists at the Jamestown site found the bones of a fish that was 14 feet (4.3 m) long!

DEADLY THIRST

Many history books report early Jamestown colonists died of hunger. However, a historian named Carville Earle suggested it wasn't hunger that killed them—it was thirst. There's a theory that most died from diseases linked to drinking **contaminated** water. Some may have died from salt poisoning, too. The river's water levels near Jamestown fell during the summer; freshwater was replaced with salty water that wasn't safe for drinking.

John Smith created a map of the Chesapeake Bay region based on his early explorations.

TENSION
BUILDS

By fall of 1608, things were finally looking up in Jamestown. John Smith had been named president of the colony, and under his leadership, colonists were at work building, repairing, and planting. Two more shipments of colonists arrived.

Smith would do anything to keep the colony going. Unfortunately, that meant stealing from native villages, which greatly angered the Powhatan people. The relations between the colonists and the Powhatans became hostile, and attacks became more common. In this strange and new world, the colonists had no **allies**.

The colony became more unstable when Smith had to leave suddenly. He was hurt in a gunpowder accident and traveled to England for medical help. He promised to send supplies. However, without his leadership, the colony faced its worst period of all.

REVEALED

John Smith wasn't liked by all at Jamestown. In fact, he was put in chains on the journey to North America for plotting against other leaders.

THE REAL JOHN SMITH

When most people hear the name "John Smith," they think of the handsome, likeable character from the Disney movie *Pocahontas*. The real John Smith became a soldier when he was only a teenager. Smith fought with the Dutch against the Spanish and with the Austrians against the Turks. As a soldier, Smith traveled from the Mediterranean to Russia and through Europe to northern Africa. His love for travel and exploration continued when he reached the New World.

The Powhatan people didn't originally see the colonists as a threat. However, after John Smith allowed his people to steal from villages, **tension** began to build.

A PERFECT DISASTER

As the winter of 1609 to 1610 set in, a great food shortage began. The winter was a disaster for Jamestown. Two of every three colonists died.

Leading up to that time, the area had experienced a drought, or long period with little rain, for 7 years. That meant there wasn't a lot of food available for anyone—natives or colonists. The colonists, unfamiliar with the land, hadn't been very successful in growing their own crops. They had once traded goods for food with the native peoples, but the hostility between them had grown.

Chief Powhatan instructed his people to kill any colonist who left Jamestown. That meant people couldn't look for food outside of their small fort.

REVEALED

Some colonists tried to leave the fort to dig up roots or find small animals to eat, but Powhatans killed them.

TOO LITTLE, TOO LATE

In June 1609, nine ships of colonists left England for Jamestown. They had enough food and supplies to help the struggling colonists. However, a **hurricane** damaged the ships. Some finally arrived in August with colonists and a few remaining supplies. The largest was wrecked near Bermuda. After 9 months, survivors of that ship built two boats out of wood from that ruined ship and set out for Jamestown again.

This artwork shows a family trying to share what little food they had in Jamestown.

THE STARVING TIME

Archaeologists have dug up some disturbing details about the period at the Jamestown site called the "Starving Time." Along with writings kept by the new Jamestown president, George Percy, these paint a troubling picture of the struggling settlement.

When the colonists first ran out of food, they ate their horses. They ate dogs and cats, and even mice and snakes. When fresh meat ran out, some colonists ate the leather from their boots and shoes. Some used starch, normally for their clothing, to make a kind of porridge. Still, many colonists died.

There were reports of **cannibalism**. Percy wrote that colonists "Licked upp the Bloode which ha[d] fallen from their weake fellowes." Some dug bodies out of graves to eat. This was the darkest point in Jamestown's history.

REVEALED

Out of the nearly 200 people who started the winter at Jamestown, only about 60 survived.

PROOF OF CANNIBALISM

It wasn't until 2013 that archaeologists found proof of cannibalism. They discovered a skull in an old trash pile. They tested the skull and found that it belonged to a 14-year-old girl from England who likely died soon after arriving; she may have come in August 1609. Her skull was chopped and cut in a way that suggested the attacker was trying to get to the girl's brain, tongue, and other soft tissue—to eat them.

The victim of cannibalism has been named Jane. Here, an expert from the Smithsonian Institution displays the actual skull and a model of what the girl might have looked like.

A POPULAR CROP

On May 24, 1610, the shipwrecked colonists finally arrived in Jamestown. What they found was horrible—few people survived the winter, and those who did were thin and ill. The group decided to leave. However, just as they were departing, more ships arrived. There were 150 new colonists onboard and a good amount of supplies. Could this struggling settlement really become a success?

John Rolfe was among the new colonists. He planted tobacco seeds that he'd found in the Caribbean. The result was a tobacco leaf that "smoked pleasant, sweete and strong," according to Ralph Hamor, secretary of Virginia. The first crops were sent to England in 1614. It was popular enough to compete in the mostly Spanish-controlled tobacco market.

REVEALED

At that time, Spain controlled Central and South America and had declared death to anyone selling tobacco seeds to a non-Spaniard. It's a mystery how John Rolfe got them.

A SEED OF SUCCESS

Archaeologists at the Jamestown site made an important discovery in 2006. They found tobacco seeds that were hundreds of years old. They may be some of the seeds that John Rolfe used to plant tobacco in the New World. This was an amazing find since tobacco seeds are tiny. They were found in a well that had been used by the colonists. Tobacco was the first successful cash crop in America.

These pieces of tobacco pipes are artifacts from the Jamestown site. Artifacts are objects left behind by people who lived long ago.

Having found a successful crop, Jamestown colonists planted more and more of it. By 1620, nearly 50,000 pounds (22,680 kg) of tobacco had been sent overseas from Jamestown. The settlement's population increased, too. By 1624, at least 6,000 people had come to Virginia. The death rate was still very high, but it was clear the colony was becoming well established.

Tobacco was good for the English, but other groups suffered for it. The English took land from the Powhatans. Unlike the native peoples, the English continued to plant on the same land each season. Also, the English planted mostly tobacco, while the natives planted small amounts of many different crops. Tobacco takes a lot of **nutrients** out of the soil it's growing in, so land is ruined for crops after a while. That led the colonists to take even more land.

SLAVERY IN JAMESTOWN

Jamestown was the first colony to use slaves in North America. Colonists needed more people to tend their fields of tobacco, and free labor would make it inexpensive to do so. Slaves first arrived in Jamestown in 1619 on a ship called the *White Lion*. It was a warship that had captured around 20 Africans from a Portuguese slave ship. The Africans became **indentured servants** at first, but African slavery had begun in the English colonies.

Many people from the tropical regions of Africa were resistant to **malaria**. This was important in the swampy, warm regions of the American South, where malaria was deadly.

As tobacco farms grew, white colonists made a profit. However, Native Americans lost their land, and Africans lost their freedom. A ship carrying slaves is pictured above.

A GROWING COLONY

Jamestown was growing quickly, without a doubt. In 1619, a ship carrying nearly 100 women arrived at Jamestown so colonists could start more families.

A growing colony required good leadership. In 1619, the first representative legislative assembly in the British American colonies was formed. It was named the Virginia House of Burgesses after the name for the representatives: burgesses.

After a few years of peace, colonists had to deal with increasing tension with native peoples. In 1622, a new chief named Opechancanough sent his men to attack Jamestown and nearby settlements. Nearly one-third of the colonists were killed in the attack. Another deadly attack happened in 1644, but the chief was captured and shot.

The Virginia Company finally lost control of the colony in 1624. Virginia, along with Jamestown, officially became a royal colony.

REVEALED

After the uprising called Bacon's Rebellion, Jamestown was rebuilt. Another fire destroyed most of it in 1698, and it was finally abandoned.

BACON'S REBELLION

Burgess Nathaniel Bacon Jr. and other colonists were angry about the decreasing price of tobacco and laws that controlled its sale. They pinned much of their anger on native peoples, who sometimes attacked farms. In 1676, Bacon assembled a group of men to attack natives. Virginia governor Sir William Berkeley punished Bacon for his actions. Then, Bacon assembled a small army to march on Jamestown, which burned to the ground. The rebellion ended after Bacon's sudden death in October 1676.

The Virginia House of Burgesses was made up of representatives who were elected by property owners.

TAKING OVER THE NEW WORLD

The English arrival at Jamestown marked a shift in the history of North America. The land—and the native peoples who lived on it—would never be the same.

Jamestown colonists introduced new animals and plants to the New World. This affected the natural ecosystems that existed there. The colonists brought livestock, such as pigs, cows, and horses. The native people didn't keep domesticated, or tame, animals. Because native people didn't fence their land, English livestock ate much of their plants, walked on their crops, and ruined the soil.

The English also brought honeybees, which spread throughout the Americas. The bees **pollinated** several kinds of plants as they went, spreading plants that were native to one region to new regions.

REVEALED

The English colonists changed the land in the New World, too. They cut down trees and native plants to create large farms called plantations.

BRINGING MALARIA

The English brought with them the worst weapon of all—disease. Among the diseases was malaria, which is spread by mosquito bites. Malaria causes people to feel tired, have difficulty breathing, and develop a bad fever. Some people survive malaria, but get sick from it repeatedly. People who have no immunity sometimes die from it. Malaria has the power to weaken people, which may have made it harder for natives to combat colonists.

Jamestown colonists remove the dead from the settlement. Death was a common occurrence in the early days of Jamestown.

POCAHONTAS: FACT VS. FICTION

Pocahontas is also an important part of the Jamestown story. However, like John Smith, the real Pocahontas is far from her character in the Disney movie of the same name.

To start, the name "Pocahontas" wasn't even her name. It was a nickname inspired by her playful character. Pocahontas's real name was Amonute, and she was sometimes called Matoaka. She was the daughter of Chief Powhatan. In the movie, she falls in love with John Smith. However, Pocahontas was only about 11 years old when the English landed.

When Pocahontas was around 14 years old, she married a man named Kocoum. Three years later, she was captured by the English and brought to Jamestown as **ransom**. She became a Christian, changed her name to Rebecca, and married John Rolfe.

REVEALED

Pocahontas followed Rolfe to England in 1616 with their son. As they prepared to return to Virginia, she became ill and died.

POCAHONTAS THE PEACEKEEPER

As the chief's daughter, Pocahontas was often used as a peacekeeper. After John Smith was captured by the Powhatans and released, Pocahontas was sent to Jamestown with him. She brought food for the hungry colonists. The young girl played in the fort with the other children. Later, because of Pocahontas's marriage to Rolfe, the English and Powhatans entered another period of peace. After her death, the relationship between the English and the Powhatans became hostile again.

John Smith claimed that Pocahontas saved his life when he was a captive of the Powhatans. It wasn't the first time Smith claimed a young woman saved his life.

JAMESTOWN HISTORICAL SITE

What happened at Jamestown shaped American history forever. During the Starving Time, it may have seemed that the settlement would fail, just as Roanoke failed years before.

The early days at Jamestown were full of challenges. Archaeologists have uncovered many of the dark details of Jamestown's past, from invasive species to cannibalism. After more than 20 years of excavations, the archaeological team at Jamestown has reconstructed what the fort might have looked like, what kinds of tools people used, and even what they ate.

There are many mysteries surrounding the early days of Jamestown. In fact, archaeologists are still hard at work at the site, unearthing new discoveries every day. Maybe one day we'll know the complete hidden history of early Jamestown.

REVEALED

In 2010, archaeologists at Jamestown discovered the site of the earliest known Protestant church in the New World. They found four graves and call these findings the "chancel burials."

JAMESTOWN REDISCOVERY

Jamestown Rediscovery is a project that began in 1994. It was launched by William Kelso, an archaeologist who first visited the area in 1963. At that time, it was assumed that the actual fort had been lost forever. It became Kelso's dream to find the fort by excavating the land. Today, you can visit Historic Jamestowne (how many colonists spelled it) and see the excavation site. Nearby, at the Rediscovery Research Center, you can see more than 2 million artifacts.

A MAP OF JAMESTOWN

blacksmith shop, bakery

second well

governor's house

1608 church

chancel burials

palisades (fence)

Jamestown Church

first well

As more discoveries are made at the Jamestown site, this map may change. For now, it helps us imagine the daily life of the people who lived there.

GLOSSARY

ally: one of two or more people or groups who work together

cannibalism: the eating of the flesh of an animal by another animal of the same kind

chancel: the part of a church that contains the altar and the seats for the priest and choir

contaminated: polluted

hurricane: an extremely large, powerful, and destructive storm with very strong winds that occurs especially in the western part of the Atlantic Ocean

incorporate: to join together

indentured servant: one who signs a contract agreeing to work for a set period of time in exchange for passage to America

malaria: a serious disease that causes chills and fever that is passed from one person to another by the bite of mosquitoes

nutrient: something a living thing needs to grow and stay alive

pollinate: to give a plant pollen from another plant of the same kind so that seeds will be produced

ransom: something that is paid in order to free someone who has been captured

tension: a state in which people or groups disagree with each other

FOR MORE INFORMATION

BOOKS

Heckt, Jackie. *The Colony of Virginia*. New York, NY: PowerKids Press, 2015.

Morley, Jacqueline. *You Wouldn't Want to Be an American Colonist! A Settlement You'd Rather Not Start*. New York, NY: Franklin Watts, 2013.

Raum, Elizabeth. *The Dreadful, Smelly Colonies: The Disgusting Details About Life in Colonial America*. Mankato, MN: Capstone Press, 2010.

WEBSITES

A Short History of Jamestown
www.nps.gov/jame/learn/historyculture/a-short-history-of-jamestown.htm
Find more facts about the English settlement.

Jamestown Rediscovery
historicjamestowne.org/education/for-kids-and-families/
Read more about the effort to uncover the hidden history of Jamestown.

INDEX